1.

pool   pan   tan

_____

_____

What is in the _____ ?

2.

far   cup   car

_____

_____

A cat is in the _____ .

3.

rake   book   bell

_____

_____

The _____ is good.

4.

bed   red   beg

_____

_____

I will go to _____ now.

Review: Decoding/Phonics (Using Letter Sounds and Context)   **DRUMS**
One word is missing from each sentence on this page. Complete the sentence so that it tells about the picture. First, circle the word you would use. Then print that word in the sentence.

Houghton Mifflin Reading, 1989 Edition

1

1

- ( ) a
- ( ) I
- ( ) in

- ( ) go
- ( ) get
- ( ) good

- ( ) look
- ( ) like
- ( ) help

2

- ( ) it
- ( ) take
- ( ) think

- ( ) here
- ( ) have
- ( ) home

- ( ) but
- ( ) out
- ( ) cat

3

- ( ) big
- ( ) is
- ( ) bear

- ( ) what
- ( ) hat
- ( ) want

- ( ) too
- ( ) do
- ( ) the

4

- ( ) not
- ( ) now
- ( ) come

- ( ) did
- ( ) to
- ( ) you

- ( ) would
- ( ) fun
- ( ) find

Review: Vocabulary Test

Find number 1. Look at the words in the first box. Find the word *I*. Mark the space for the word. (Continue in this manner, pronouncing the words to be tested.)

DRUMS

2

Houghton Mifflin Reading, 1989 Edition

Review: Comprehension (Predicting Outcomes)
The first two pictures in each box show the beginning of a story. Look at the pictures. Then find the picture that shows what will probably happen next. Circle that picture.

DRUMS

Houghton Mifflin Reading, 1989 Edition

Review: Comprehension (Understanding Cause-Effect Relationships)

DRUMS

Look at the first picture in each box. It shows something that happened. Find the picture that shows why the thing happened, or what caused it to happen. Circle the picture.

Houghton Mifflin Reading, 1989 Edition

1.

2.

3. See the hat.

I like **this.**

4. Here is a cat.

Here   a cat   you

Would you like **this?**

1.

See the big hat.

You can have **this.**

2.

I like the bear.

I will get **this.**

3.

Here is a home.

This is a good home.

4.

Here is a big cat.

Do you want **this?**

6

Comprehension: Word Referent *this*
Read each pair of sentences. A word in the second sentence is in heavy black letters. Think about the meaning of the word. Then circle the words in the first sentence that the word in heavy black letters stands for.

DRUMS

Houghton Mifflin Reading, 1989 Edition

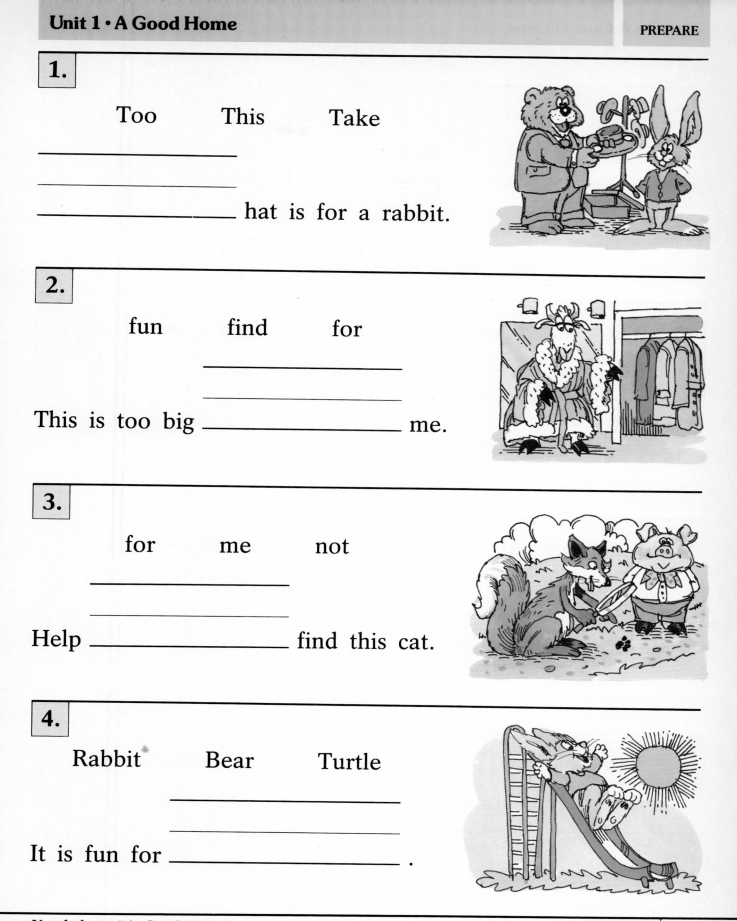

1.

Too   This   Take

_____

_____

_____ hat is for a rabbit.

2.

fun   find   for

_____

_____

This is too big _____ me.

3.

for   me   not

_____

_____

Help _____ find this cat.

4.

Rabbit   Bear   Turtle

_____

_____

It is fun for _____ .

Vocabulary: "A Good Home"
One word is missing from each sentence on this page. Complete the sentence so that it tells about the picture. First, circle the word you would use. Then print that word in the sentence.

DRUMS

7

1.

But it is too big!

This is not the home for me.

A.

_____

2.

It is a good home for a bear.

But it is not good for a rabbit.

B.

_____

3.

I can not get in it!

What will I do now, Turtle?

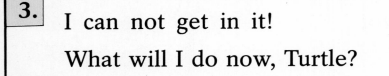

C.

_____

4.

I think I like it here.

This is the home for me.

D.

_____

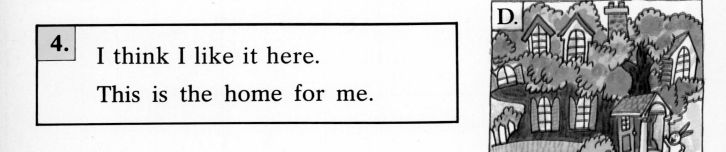

Comprehension: "A Good Home"   DRUMS
The sentences on this page are things Rabbit said in the story "A Good Home." Read the sentences in each box. Then find the picture that goes with the sentences. Print the letter of the picture on the line under the box.

Houghton Mifflin Reading, 1989 Edition

1.

hen   hem   heat

Here is a _____ .

2.

cup   cut   came

I will _____ it for you.

3.

rug   rub   run

This rabbit can _____ .

4.

pet   peg   pen

I want a _____ , too.

5.

bag   bad   bat

You can have this _____ .

Decoding/Phonics: End Sounds *n*, *t*
One word is missing from each sentence on this page. Complete the sentence so that it tells about the picture. Circle the word you would use.

DRUMS

Houghton Mifflin Reading, 1989 Edition

1.

You can get a cat here.

I want a hat, too.

2.

I want to go home now.

This is fun.

3.

Rabbit is too big.

This will help you get it.

4.

This is good for you.

You can not go out now.

Comprehension: Drawing Conclusions
Look at each picture and read the sentences to the right. Decide which sentence tells what you think the character in the picture is saying. Underline the sentence.

DRUMS

Houghton Mifflin Reading, 1989 Edition

1.

The **rabbits** like it here.

2.

The **hat** is too big.

3.

It is fun to see the **bears**.

4.

Can you find the **cats**?

Decoding: Plurals

Read each sentence. Think about what the word in heavy black letters means. Then circle the picture that goes with the sentence.

DRUMS

Houghton Mifflin Reading, 1989 Edition

1.

The **bus** will take you home.

2.

I will help the **cook**.

3.

What is in the **cup**?

4.

Max is a **king** now.

Decoding/Phonics: Using Letter Sounds and Context
Read each sentence. The word in heavy black letters is new. Use the sounds for the letters and the sense of the other words to figure it out. Then look at the three pictures below the sentence. Circle the one that the new word names.

DRUMS

Houghton Mifflin Reading, 1989 Edition

1.

I will get a hat.

We want to go out.

The cat will like **it.**

2.

The rabbit is in a hat.

Max will take **it** out.

Comprehension: Word Referents *I, we, it*　　　DRUMS

Top: Read the three sentences in box *1*. Think about what the words in heavy black letters mean. Draw a line from each sentence to the picture that goes with it. *Bottom:* Read the two sentences in box *2*. Think about what the word *it* means. Circle the words that *it* stands for.

Houghton Mifflin Reading, 1989 Edition

13

1.

2.

cat   home   rabbit

_____

_____

_____

Help Bear get home.

Help Rabbit get home.

Help Turtle get home, too.

Comprehension: Following Directions

DRUMS

Read the sentences at the top of the page. Then follow these directions. *1.* Circle the bear. Then draw a line from the bear to the cave. *2.* Underline the rabbit. Then draw a line from the rabbit to the rabbit hole. *3.* Circle *and* underline the turtle. Then draw a line from the turtle to the pond.

1.

Bear is here.

Rabbit is here.

Are the animals here?

_____

_____

_____

2.

Do your work, Bear.

Do your work, Rabbit.

Do the animals work?

_____

_____

_____

Vocabulary: "Think Big!" (Part One)
Look at each picture, and read the sentences in the speech balloons. Then read each question. Print a sentence that answers the question. Use the same words that are in the question.

DRUMS

Houghton Mifflin Reading, 1989 Edition

1.

What did Pam do?

2.

What did Pam want to see?

3.

Did Pam see the bears?

_____

_____

Pam did _____ .

Comprehension: ''Think Big!'' (Part One)
The questions on this page are about the story ''Think Big!'' Read each question. For 1 and 2, circle the picture that shows the answer. For 3, print the rest of a sentence to answer the question.

DRUMS

Houghton Mifflin Reading, 1989 Edition

1.

for   fun   find

_____

_____

This is not _____ me.

2.

you   out   are

_____

_____

The bears _____ home.

3.

your   will   we

_____

_____

Is this _____ hat?

4.

what   work   this

_____

_____

Rabbits _____ here.

Vocabulary Reinforcement   DRUMS
One word is missing from each sentence on this page. Complete the sentence so that it tells about
the picture. First, circle the word you would use. Then print that word in the sentence.

Houghton Mifflin Reading, 1989 Edition

1.

I will get in the **boat**.

2.

Did you find your **pen**?

3.

What is in the **jar**?

4.

A **mop** will help you do your work.

Decoding/Phonics: Using Letter Sounds and Context

DRUMS

Read each sentence. The word in heavy black letters is new. Use the sounds for the letters and the sense of the other words to figure it out. Then look at the three pictures below the sentence. Circle the one that the new word names.

Houghton Mifflin Reading, 1989 Edition

Where	be	Little	and

1.

_____

_____

Come here _____ help!

2.

_____

_____

_____ is Little Bear?

3.

_____

_____

Can Little Bear _____ here?

4.

_____

_____

_____ Bear is here!

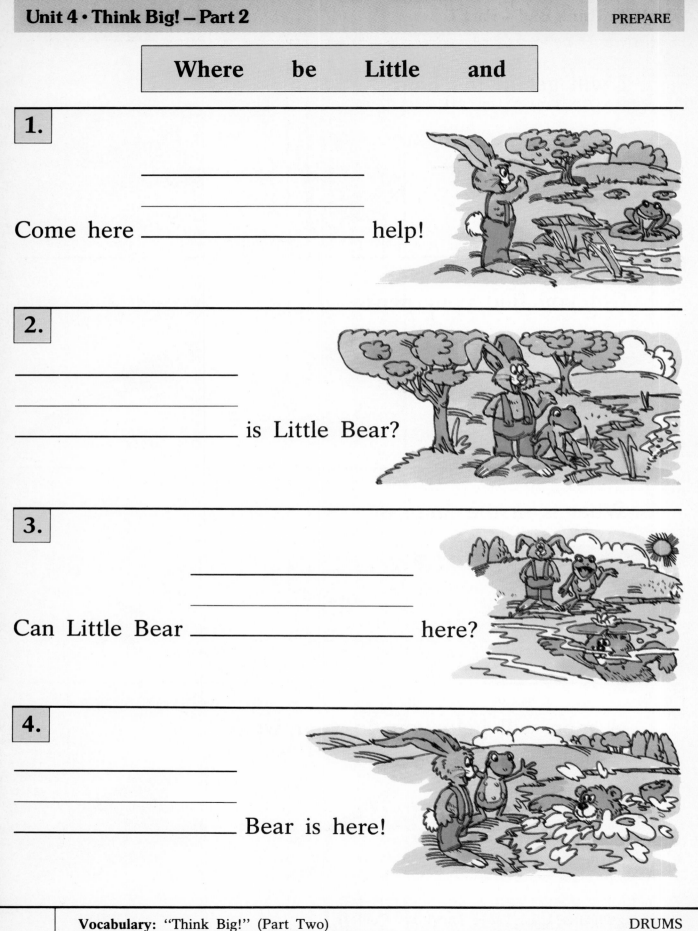

20

Vocabulary: "Think Big!" (Part Two)
One word is missing from each sentence on this page. Complete the sentence so that it tells about the picture. Choose from the words at the top of the page. Print the word in the sentence.

DRUMS

Houghton Mifflin Reading, 1989 Edition

A.

1. You can work in here, Pam.
This is where the turtles are.

_____

B.

2. Take a look here, Pam.
This is where the rabbits are.

_____

C.

3. This is where the cats are.
I see little cats and big cats.

_____

D.

4. Now this is big!
It is not a bear.
But Pam will like this!

_____

Comprehension: "Think Big!" (Part Two)   DRUMS
The sentences on this page are things Ana said in the story "Think Big!" Read the sentences in each box. Then find the picture that goes with the sentences. Print the letter of the picture on the line under the box.

Houghton Mifflin Reading, 1989 Edition

1.

It can go.

2.

It can help you to see.

3.

It is in a home.

4.

It can help you work.

Comprehension: Categorizing
Read the sentence in each box. Then look at the four pictures. Decide which three pictures belong together, and then circle them.

DRUMS

Houghton Mifflin Reading, 1989 Edition

1

- ○ now
- ○ and
- ○ are

- ○ be
- ○ big
- ○ but

- ○ look
- ○ little
- ○ like

2

- ○ can
- ○ see
- ○ are

- ○ where
- ○ what
- ○ bear

- ○ want
- ○ home
- ○ work

3

- ○ your
- ○ out
- ○ you

- ○ fun
- ○ for
- ○ your

- ○ rabbit
- ○ think
- ○ help

4

- ○ me
- ○ be
- ○ get

- ○ to
- ○ the
- ○ this

- ○ good
- ○ too
- ○ would

Vocabulary Test
Find number 1. Look at the words in the first box. Find the word *and*. Mark the space for the word.
(Continue in this manner, pronouncing the words to be tested.)

DRUMS

Houghton Mifflin Reading, 1989 Edition

1.

_____ The bears find hats.

_____ The bears look for hats.

_____ The bears go out.

2.

_____ The turtles have fun.

_____ The turtles get out.

_____ The turtles go in.

Comprehension: Noting Correct Sequence

DRUMS

Houghton Mifflin Reading, 1989 Edition

1.

_____ Max and I will have fun.

_____ I go out.

_____ I find Max.

2.

_____ I take the turtle home.

_____ I get the turtle to go in a hat.

_____ I find a little turtle.

Comprehension: Noting Correct Sequence

DRUMS

Read the sentences below the picture. Put *1* before the sentence that tells what happens first, *2* before the sentence that tells what happens next, and *3* before the sentence that tells what happens last.

Houghton Mifflin Reading, 1989 Edition

25

1.

Do you see the **turtles**?

2.

This is for the **rabbit**.

3.

Here are the **hats.**

4.

Where are the **cats**?

Decoding: Plurals
Read each sentence. Think about what the word in heavy black letters means. Then circle the picture that goes with the sentence.

DRUMS

Houghton Mifflin Reading, 1989 Edition

1.

Help me find the cat.

_____ I can not find the cat.

_____ I do not like the cat.

2.

Take this hat to Pam.

_____ It is not a good hat.

_____ It is a good hat for Pam.

3.

I want Max to see this.

_____ Animals are fun.

_____ Max will like this.

Comprehension: Understanding Cause-Effect Relationships

Look at the picture and read what the person says. Decide which of the two sentences tells why the person said that. Put an X by the sentence.

DRUMS

1. _____ ag

2. _____ ame

3. It is **flat** now.

4. Do you see the **frog**?

fly   fill

_____

5. It can _____ .

fun   frown

_____

6. What a _____ !

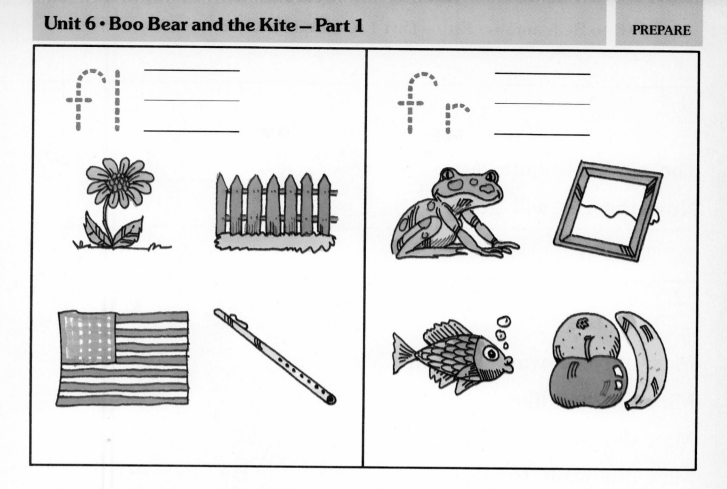

1. Bear will **fly.**

2. Turtle can **frame** it.

Decoding/Phonics: Clusters *fl, fr*

Top: Trace and print the letters *fl* and *fr.* Now listen as I name each picture. (Name the pictures in each box.) Circle the pictures whose names begin with the sounds for *fl* or *fr. Bottom:* Read each sentence. The word in heavy black letters is new! Circle the picture that goes with the sentence.

1.

The cat will come here.
Now the cat will go.

2.

Max did not want to come here.
Max did not like it.
Max did not have fun.
Max did want to go home.

Max   home

3.

The bears get hats.
Now the bears take a look.
The bears like the hats.
The hats are fun!

hats for rabbits   hats for bears

| a home for Pam   a home for Rabbit |

1. This is a home.

It is not a home for you.

It is a home for Rabbit.

It is not big.

It is a good home.

_____

_____

2. This is a home, too.

It is a home for Pam.

It is a big home.

Pam will like it here.

_____

_____

Comprehension: Getting the Topic   DRUMS
Read each story. Print *a home for Pam* under the story that tells about a home for Pam. Print *a home for Rabbit* under the story that tells about a home for Rabbit.

Houghton Mifflin Reading, 1989 Edition

1.

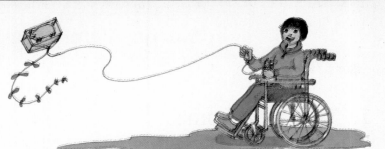

My kite is like a pig.

My kite is like a rabbit.

2.

It is a good day to fly my kite.

It is a good day to see my friend.

3.

I will find a home for the cat.

I will make a kite for my friend.

4.

My friend and I make a pig.

My friend and I make hats.

5.

My friend will fly home.

My friend will fly a kite.

Vocabulary: "Boo Bear and the Kite" (Part One)   **DRUMS**
Read the two sentences by each picture. Decide which sentence tells about the picture. Underline that sentence.

Houghton Mifflin Reading, 1989 Edition

1.

Boo would like to fly the kite.

Boo would like to make the kite.

2.

Boo can make the kite fly.

Boo can not make the kite fly.

3.

Pig would like to help Boo.

Turtle would like to help Boo.

4.

Pig can not get the kite to fly.

Pig can make the kite fly.

5.

Is it a good day for Boo and Pig?

It is
.

Comprehension: "Boo Bear and the Kite" (Part One)
Think about the story "Boo Bear and the Kite." For 1 through 4, read the two sentences in each box. Circle the sentence that is true. For 5, trace the letters and print the rest of a sentence that answers the question. (If necessary, refer children to *Drums* page 25.)

DRUMS

Houghton Mifflin Reading, 1989 Edition

1.

fly　　　day

_____

_____

My kite can _____ .

2.

and　　　are

_____

_____

Where _____ my friends?

3.

little　　　like

_____

_____

It is a good _____ pig.

4.

take　　　make

_____

_____

I can _____ it work.

Vocabulary Reinforcement
One word is missing from each sentence on this page. Complete the sentence so that it tells about the picture.
First, circle the word you would use. Then print that word in the sentence.

DRUMS

Houghton Mifflin Reading, 1989 Edition

1.

doll   dog   dot

What did the little _____ find?

2.

bed   beg   bell

You are in my _____ !

3.

sag   sat   sad

This little pig is _____ .

4.

hid   hit   hill

This little rabbit _____ .

5.

bad   bat   bag

What is in the _____ ?

Decoding/Phonics: End Sounds *g, d*
One word is missing from each sentence on this page. Complete the sentence so that it tells about the picture. Circle the word you would use.

DRUMS

Houghton Mifflin Reading, 1989 Edition

1. get ═══

2. like ═══

3. Rabbit makes a kite.

4. Tiny thinks it is good.

see　　　sees

_____

_____

5. Bear _____ a turtle.

Decoding: Verbs with *s* Ending

DRUMS

Houghton Mifflin Reading, 1989 Edition

1.

Ana wants to fly a kite.

Ana makes a friend.

2.

The turtle sees a cat.

The turtle gets a hat.

3.

Max takes the cat out.

Max comes home now.

4.

The rabbit helps a friend.

The rabbit likes it here.

5.

The pig looks in the can.

The pig likes the cat.

Decoding: Verbs with *s* Ending

Read the two sentences by each picture. Decide which sentence tells about the picture. Underline that sentence.

DRUMS

Houghton Mifflin Reading, 1989 Edition

1. bo___

2. six

3. fox

4.

fix   far

_____

_____

I will _____ it.

5.

wag   wax

_____

_____

Did you _____ it?

1.

foot   fox   fog

This is a _____ .

2.

mix   mill   miss

Will you help _____ , Ana?

3.

fix   fit   fine

Pam can _____ the kite.

4.

bowl   box   boat

This _____ is for you.

5.

ax   at   am

Do you want my _____ ?

Decoding/Phonics: Sound Association for *x*
One word is missing from each sentence on this page. Complete the sentence so that it tells about the picture. Circle the word you would use.

DRUMS

Houghton Mifflin Reading, 1989 Edition

39

Fox   tail   needs

_____
_____

1. Bear _____ help.

_____
_____

2. _____ will help Bear.

_____
_____

3. Fox will make the _____ .

Vocabulary: "Boo Bear and the Kite" (Part Two)
Read the story at the top of the page. Then decide which word you would use to complete each sentence at the bottom. Print a word in each sentence. Use the words from the box.

DRUMS

Houghton Mifflin Reading, 1989 Edition

1.

Boo and Pig can not fly the kite.

The kite is too big.

The kite needs a tail.

2.

Boo wants Fox to fly the kite.

Boo thinks Fox can do it.

Boo thinks Fox is too little.

3.

Boo and Pig can fly the kite.

Fox makes a tail for the kite.

Fox makes a little kite for Boo and Pig.

Comprehension: "Boo Bear and the Kite" (Part Two)   DRUMS
Think about the story "Boo Bear and the Kite." Read the three sentences in each box. The first sentence
tells something that happens in the story. One of the other two sentences tells *why* it happens. Underline
that sentence.   Houghton Mifflin Reading, 1989 Edition   **41**

1.

rock   road   ring

Where will this ____ take me?

2.

sit   six   sill

Rabbit will ____ here.

3.

farm   fig   fan

I will take this ____ home.

4.

web   win   wig

I like my ____ !

Decoding/Phonics: End Sounds   DRUMS
One word is missing from each sentence on this page. Complete the sentence so that it tells about the picture. Circle the word you would use.

Houghton Mifflin Reading, 1989 Edition

1.

_____ I take my kite out.

_____ I fly my kite.

_____ I make a kite.

2.

_____ I find Max.

_____ I look for Max.

_____ I make Max look good.

Comprehension: Noting Correct Sequence

Read the sentences below the picture. Put _1_ before the sentence that tells what happens first, _2_ before the sentence that tells what happens next, and _3_ before the sentence that tells what happens last.

DRUMS

Houghton Mifflin Reading, 1989 Edition

1.

Pig **can't** see now.

did not   can not

2.

Where's my cat?

What is   Where is

3.

The rabbits **aren't** here now.

are not   is not

4.

Here's your kite.

It is   Here is

Decoding: Contractions with *'s, n't*
Read each sentence and the words below it. Decide which two words were put together to make the word in heavy black letters. Underline those two words. Then circle the picture that goes with the sentence.

DRUMS

Houghton Mifflin Reading, 1989 Edition

1.

frog   flag   log

I want a little _____ , too.

2.

foot   front   round

This is the _____ !

3.

late   fat   flat

It's _____ , isn't it?

4.

flower   fruit   lower

Do you want a _____ ?

5.

frame   game   farm

Help me make a _____ for it.

Decoding/Phonics: Clusters *fl, fr*   DRUMS
One word is missing from each sentence on this page. Complete the sentence so that it tells about the picture. Circle the word you would use.

Houghton Mifflin Reading, 1989 Edition   **45**

1. Look, Ana!

Do you see the kites?

I like the big kite.

But it needs a tail.

Now I see a little kite.

The little kite can fly.

I think kites are fun!

tails	kites

---

2. You have a hat.

I have a hat, too.

Your hat looks like a bear.

It is a good hat.

My hat looks like a rabbit.

What fun hats can be!

hats	bears

Comprehension: Getting the Topic   DRUMS
Read each story. Then read the words in the box. Circle the word that tells what the story is about.

Houghton Mifflin Reading, 1989 Edition

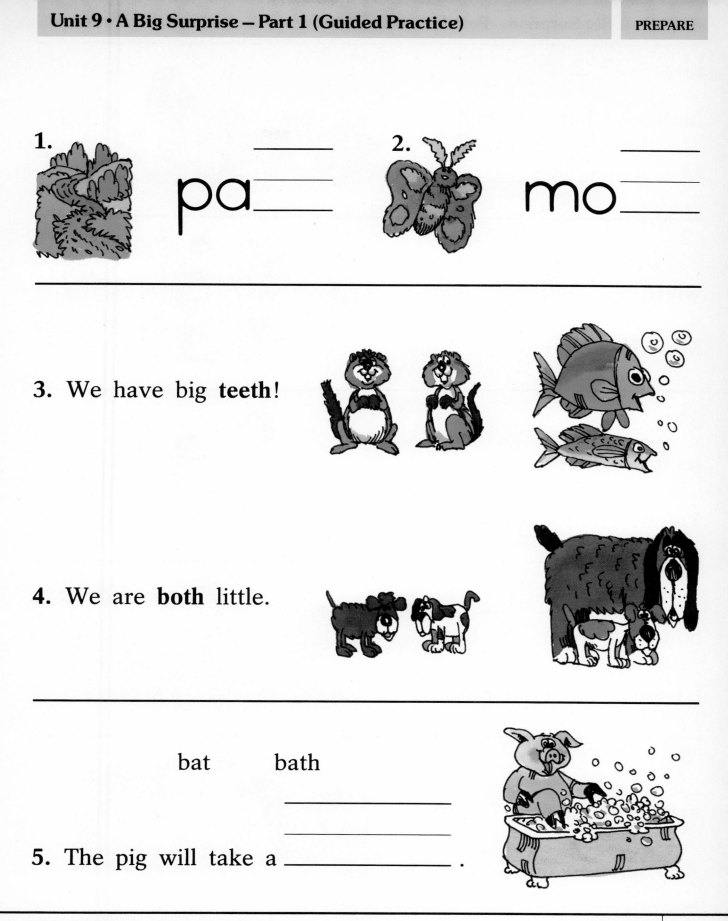

1. pa_____

2. mo_____

3. We have big **teeth**!

4. We are **both** little.

bat   bath

_____

5. The pig will take a _____ .

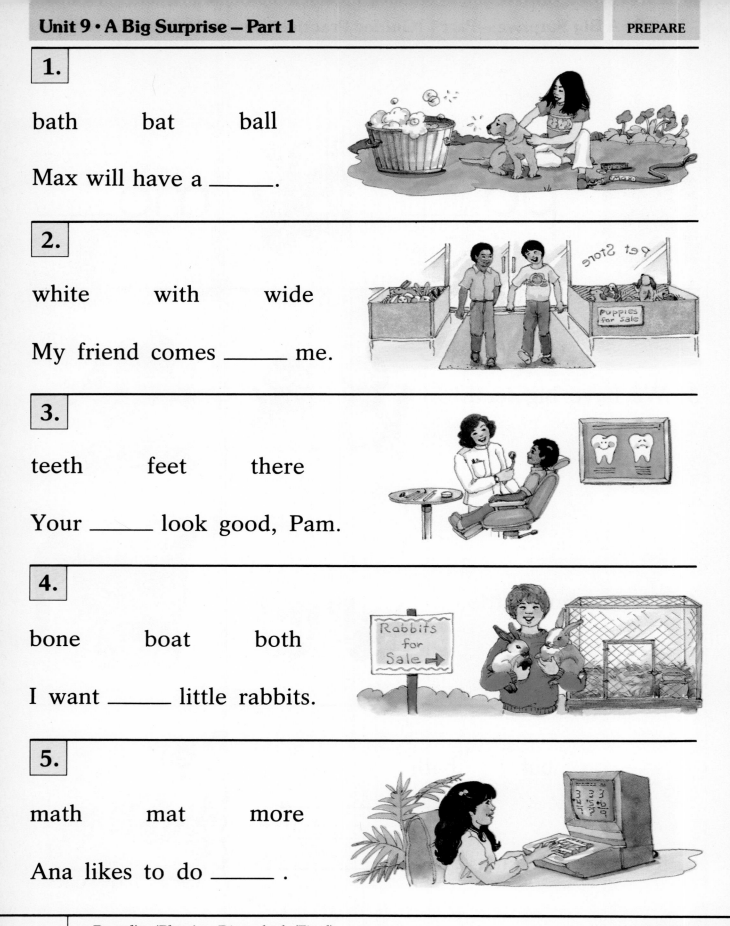

1.

bath   bat   ball

Max will have a _____.

2.

white   with   wide

My friend comes _____ me.

3.

teeth   feet   there

Your _____ look good, Pam.

4.

bone   boat   both

I want _____ little rabbits.

5.

math   mat   more

Ana likes to do _____ .

Decoding/Phonics: Digraph *th* (Final)
One word is missing from each sentence on this page. Complete the sentence so that it tells about the picture. Circle the word you would use.

DRUMS

Houghton Mifflin Reading, 1989 Edition

surprise
with
that
at

John: Look _____ that big cat, Mother.

Mother: I see _____ big cat, John.

I see little cats, too.

John: What a _____ !

The big cat is a mother.

The mother is _____ the little cats.

Vocabulary: "A Big Surprise" (Part One)   DRUMS
Look at the picture. Then complete the sentences so that they tell a story about the picture. Use the words in the box.

Houghton Mifflin Reading, 1989 Edition

1.

It is a big day for ____ .

John   Mother

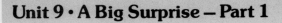

2.

John likes ____ .

rabbits   surprises

3.

John wants ____ to come, too.

Gramps   a friend

4.

Gramps is at ____ .

work   home

5.

Mother and John go to ____ .

see the bears   where Gramps works

Comprehension: "A Big Surprise" (Part One)
The sentences on this page tell about the story "A Big Surprise." But the sentences are not complete.
Circle the word or words you would use to complete each sentence.

DRUMS

Houghton Mifflin Reading, 1989 Edition

1.

The rabbit looks at me.

The rabbit helps me.

2.

Max looks for work.

Max works and works.

3.

Gramps likes to have fun.

Gramps makes me a kite.

4.

Mother surprises Will.

Mother comes to get Will.

5.

Ana gets a big bear.

Ana sees a big bear.

Decoding: Verbs with *s* Ending
Read the two sentences by each picture. Decide which sentence tells about the picture. Underline that sentence.

DRUMS

1

- ○ are
- ○ at
- ○ and

- ○ where
- ○ would
- ○ mother

- ○ surprise
- ○ see
- ○ rabbit

2

- ○ the
- ○ hat
- ○ that

- ○ we
- ○ with
- ○ what

- ○ need
- ○ now
- ○ find

3

- ○ tail
- ○ will
- ○ that

- ○ cat
- ○ did
- ○ day

- ○ my
- ○ fly
- ○ for

4

- ○ find
- ○ fox
- ○ friend

- ○ make
- ○ kite
- ○ take

- ○ but
- ○ pig
- ○ big

Vocabulary Test
Find number 1. Look at the words in the first box. Find the word *at*. Mark the space for the word. (Continue in this manner, pronouncing the words to be tested.)

DRUMS

Houghton Mifflin Reading, 1989 Edition

5. Mother Turtle   Little Turtle

6. Rabbit   Fox

7. I will help you.   You are too little.

8. It is a good day! I have a big surprise!

Pig makes a home.

It is not a good home.

Fox can get in.

Fox wants Pig!

1. The home is not ____ .

       day   good   fun

2. ____ can get in.

       Fox   Bear   Cat

Pig works and works.

Pig makes a good home.

Fox can not get in now.

Fox will not get Pig.

3. Pig makes a good ____ .

       hat   friend   home

4. Fox will not get ____ .

       Pig   Bear   Cat

Comprehension: Noting Important Details
Read the story in each box. Then read each sentence below the story. Circle the word that correctly completes each sentence.

DRUMS

Houghton Mifflin Reading, 1989 Edition

1.

tell   more   may

_____

_____

Help me make some _____ !

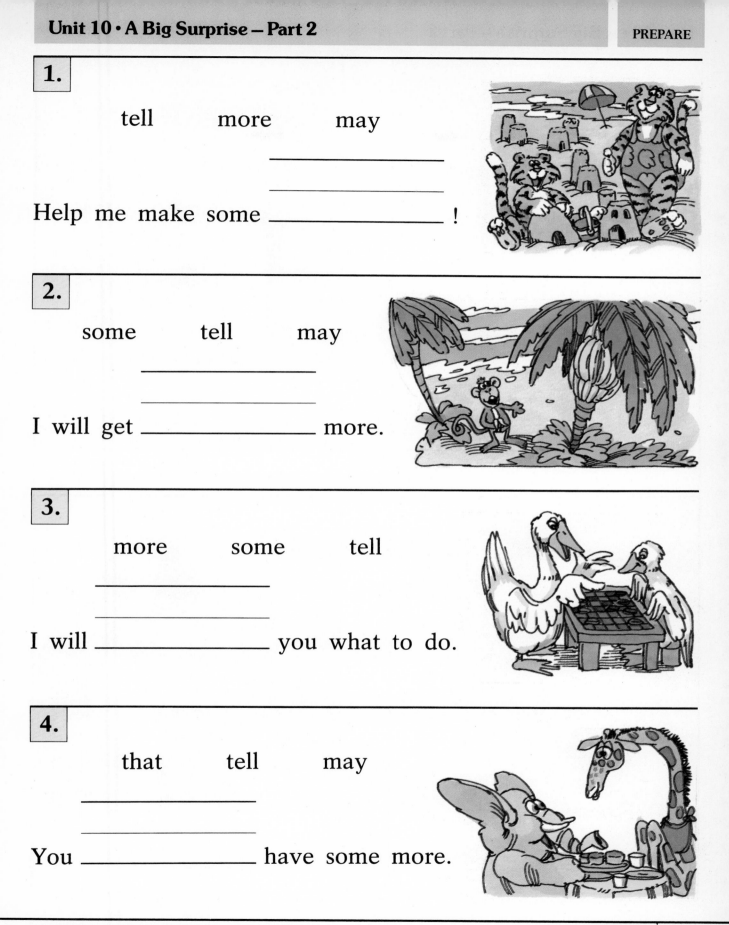

2.

some   tell   may

_____

_____

I will get _____ more.

3.

more   some   tell

_____

_____

I will _____ you what to do.

4.

that   tell   may

_____

_____

You _____ have some more.

Vocabulary: "A Big Surprise" (Part Two)   DRUMS

One word is missing from each sentence on this page. Complete the sentence so that it tells about the picture. First, circle the word you would use. Then print that word in the sentence.

Houghton Mifflin Reading, 1989 Edition

55

_____

_____

_____

_____

Comprehension: "A Big Surprise" (Part Two)

DRUMS

The pictures on this page are from the story "A Big Surprise." Look at the pictures. Then put the number _1, 2, 3_ or _4_ below each picture to show the order in which things happen in the story.

56

Houghton Mifflin Reading, 1989 Edition

1.

Do you like my turtle?

You can have **this.**

2.

I will make a tail.

This is for my kite.

3.

See the pig.

This is for Pam.

4.

What a good surprise!

Is **this** for me?

Comprehension: Word Referent *this*   DRUMS

Read each pair of sentences. A word in the second sentence is in heavy black letters. Think about the meaning of the word. Then circle the words in the first sentence that the word in heavy black letters stands for.

Houghton Mifflin Reading, 1989 Edition

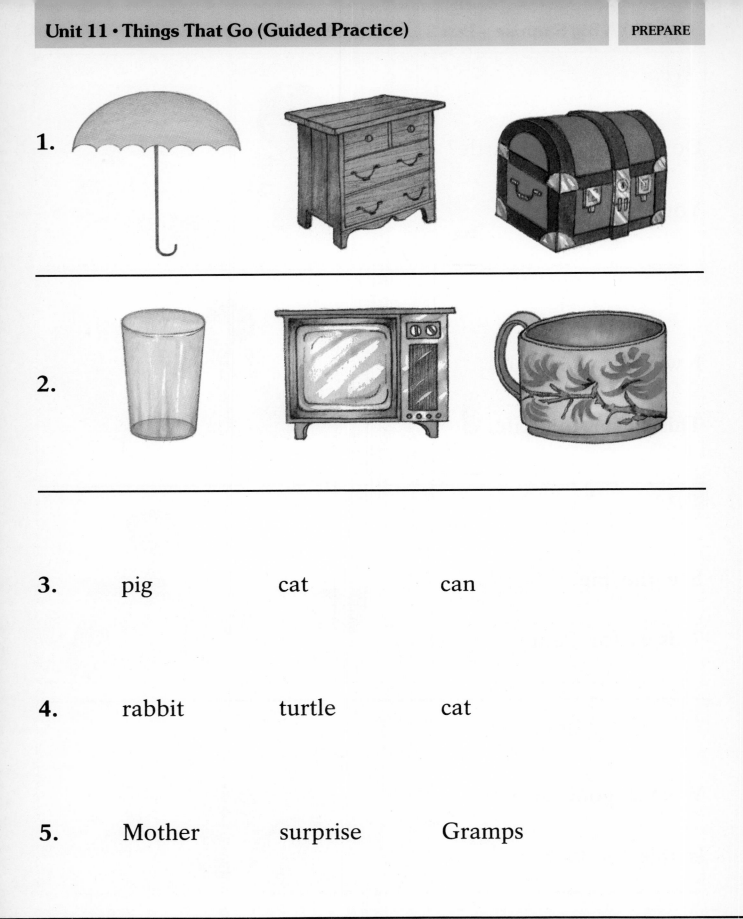

1.

2.

3.   pig   cat   can

4.   rabbit   turtle   cat

5.   Mother   surprise   Gramps

1.

We have tails.

2.

It can fly.

3.

It is a hat.

4.

It is a home.

Comprehension: Categorizing
Read the sentence in each box. Then look at the four pictures. Decide which three pictures belong together, and then circle them.

DRUMS

Houghton Mifflin Reading, 1989 Edition

1.

may   more   need

_____

_____

You _____ have some.

2.

works   needs   where

_____

_____

My pig _____ a tail.

3.

are   be   at

_____

_____

John looks _____ the fox.

4.

day   and   are

_____

_____

My friend _____ I work.

Vocabulary: "Things That Go"
One word is missing from each sentence on this page. Complete the sentence so that it tells about the picture. First, circle the word you would use. Then print that word in the sentence.

DRUMS

Houghton Mifflin Reading, 1989 Edition

1.

You can fly in this.

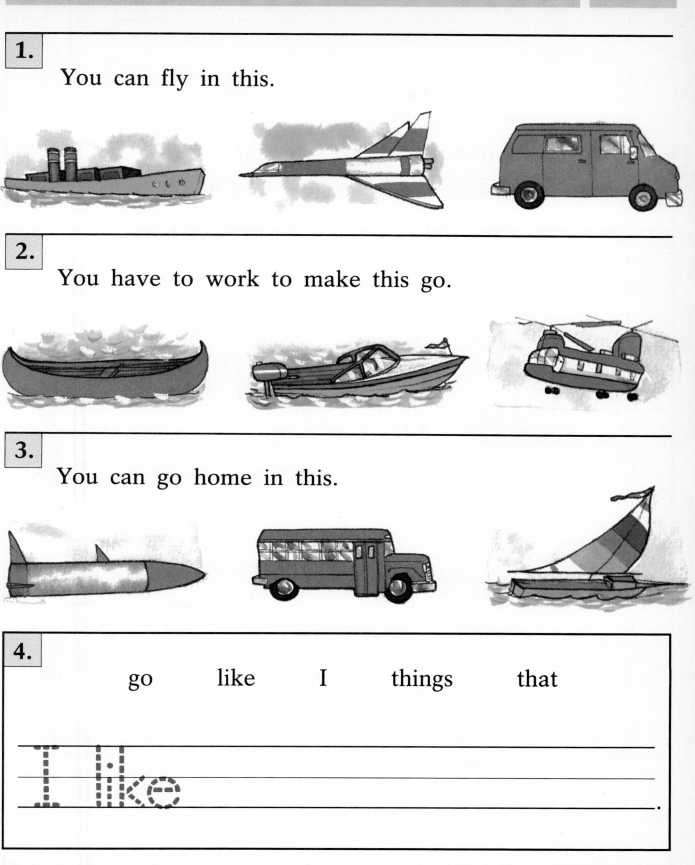

2.

You have to work to make this go.

3.

You can go home in this.

4.

| go | like | I | things | that |

I like

Comprehension: "Things That Go"
Think about "Things That Go" as you do this page. For 1 through 3, read each sentence. Circle the picture that goes with the sentence. For 4, put the words in order to make a sentence. Print your sentence in the lines. Trace the dotted lines to start the sentence.

DRUMS

Houghton Mifflin Reading, 1989 Edition

61

1. Pig can't see Rabbit.

2. It isn't a good day.

3. Where's your hat, Turtle?

4. Here's a surprise for you, Rabbit.

5. Bear didn't have a home to go to.

6. What's in your can?

Decoding: Contractions with 's, n't
Read each sentence. Underline the word that was made by putting two words together. Then find the picture that goes with the sentence. Print the number of the sentence under the picture.

DRUMS

Houghton Mifflin Reading, 1989 Edition

1.

pat   past   path

Here is the _____ to my home.

2.

tears   teeth   tent

What big _____ you have!

3.

math   most   mat

I need help with my _____ .

4.

both   boast   bell

Bear, you can't have _____ !

5.

bath   boat   back

I will take a _____ now.

Decoding/Phonics: Digraph *th* (Final)
One word is missing from each sentence on this page. Complete the sentence so that it tells about the picture. Circle the word you would use.

DRUMS

1.

What do you think Gramps will do?

Gramps will go home now.

Gramps will not get in.

2.

What do you think Pam will do?

Pam will get a surprise.

Pam will fly the kite.

3.

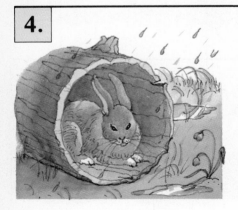

What do you think John will do?

John will take the cat out.

John will surprise Mother.

4.

What do you think the rabbit will do?

The rabbit will not go out now.

The rabbit will find a friend.

Comprehension: "Predicting Outcomes"   DRUMS
Look at the picture and read the question. Underline the sentence that answers the question.

Houghton Mifflin Reading, 1989 Edition

Turtle likes to fly kites.
Turtle can't fly this kite.
This kite is too big for Turtle.
Turtle needs a little kite.

1. Turtle can't _____ this kite.

   fly   have   help

2. The kite is too _____ for Turtle.

   big   little   good

Here is a surprise for Turtle.
It is a little kite.
Turtle can fly this kite.
Now Turtle can have fun.

3. The surprise is a little _____ .

   hat   kite   friend

4. It is a kite that _____ can fly.

   Turtle   Rabbit   Tiny

Comprehension: Noting Important Details
Read the story in each box. Then read the sentences below each story. Circle the word that correctly completes each sentence.

DRUMS

1. _____ est

2. pea _____

3. This is my **chin**.

4. We are at the **beach**.

cap   chop

_____
_____

5. Mother will _____ it.

reach   real

_____
_____

6. John can't _____ it.

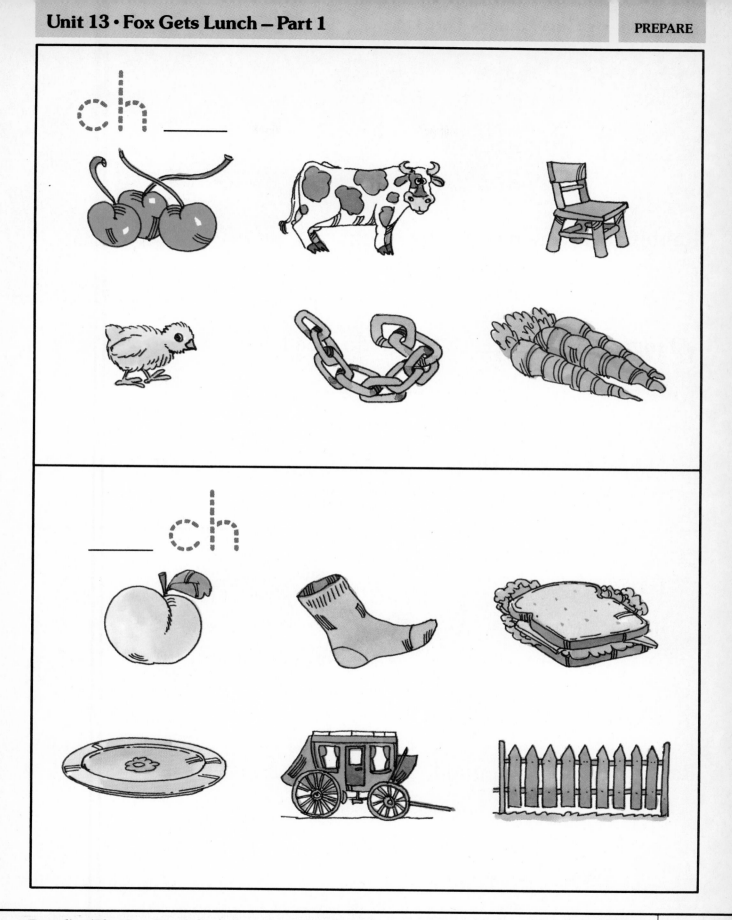

Decoding/Phonics: Digraph *ch* (Initial and Final)
Listen as I name each picture. (Name the pictures in each box.) Now trace the letters *ch* in each box. In the top box, circle the pictures whose names *begin* with the sound for *ch*. In the bottom box, circle the pictures whose names *end* with the sound for *ch*.

DRUMS

Houghton Mifflin Reading, 1989 Edition

67

Yes
red

Rabbit: Do you need help, Frog?

_____

_____

Frog: _____ , I do need help.

_____

_____

I need some _____ .

Will you get some red for me?

Frog
lunch

_____

_____

Rabbit: That looks good, _____ .

_____

_____

Now we can have _____ !

Vocabulary: "Fox Gets Lunch" (Part One)
Look at the picture at the top of the page. Then complete the sentences so that they tell about the picture. Use the words in the box. Then do the bottom of the page the same way.

DRUMS

Houghton Mifflin Reading, 1989 Edition

1.

What did Fox look like?

a big red frog

a little bear

2.

What did Fox want?

frogs for lunch

rabbits for lunch

3.

What did Little Rabbit tell Mother?

A big red frog wants to come in.

A big red fox is here.

4.

What did Mother tell Little Rabbit?

Frogs aren't red!

Frogs can not have lunch here.

5.

What will Mother Rabbit do?

make a surprise lunch for Fox

tell Fox to go home

Comprehension: "Fox Gets Lunch" (Part One)   DRUMS
The questions on this page are about the story "Fox Gets Lunch." Read each question. Underline the answer.

Houghton Mifflin Reading, 1989 Edition

1.

I will have a **pear** with my lunch.

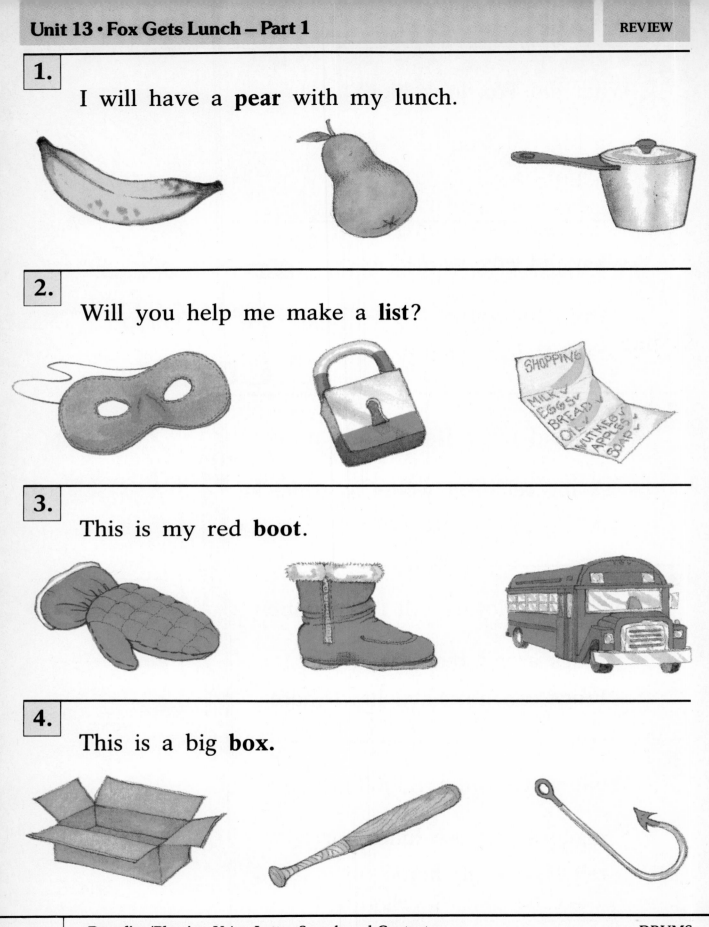

2.

Will you help me make a **list**?

3.

This is my red **boot**.

4.

This is a big **box.**

Decoding/Phonics: Using Letter Sounds and Context   DRUMS
Read each sentence. The word in heavy black letters is new. Use the sounds for the letters and the sense of the other words to figure it out. Then look at the three pictures below the sentence. Circle the one that the new word names.   Houghton Mifflin Reading, 1989 Edition

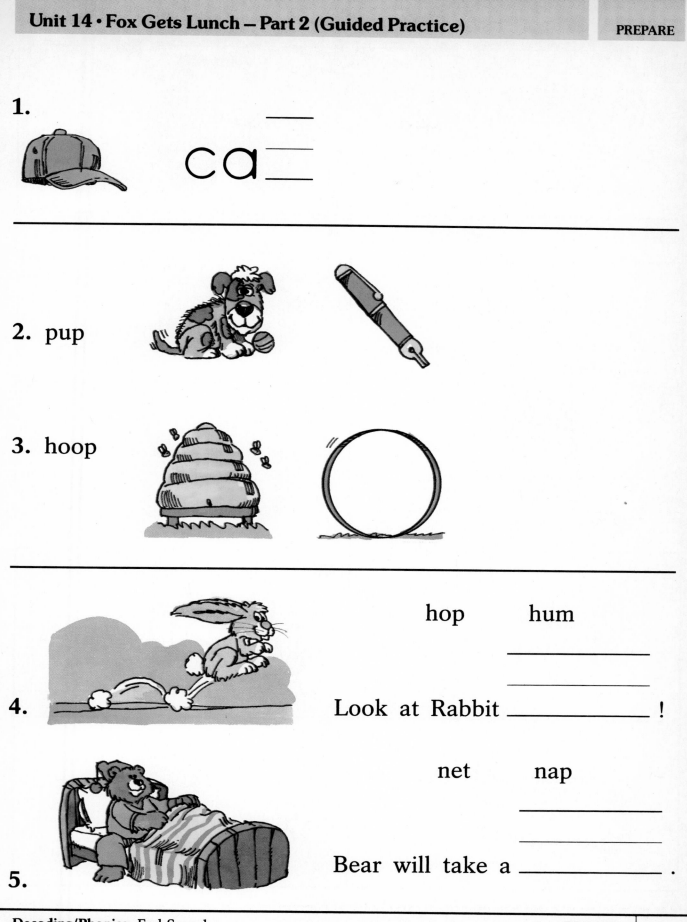

1.

ca__

2. pup

3. hoop

hop   hum

_____

_____

4.

Look at Rabbit _____ !

net   nap

_____

_____

Bear will take a _____ .

5.

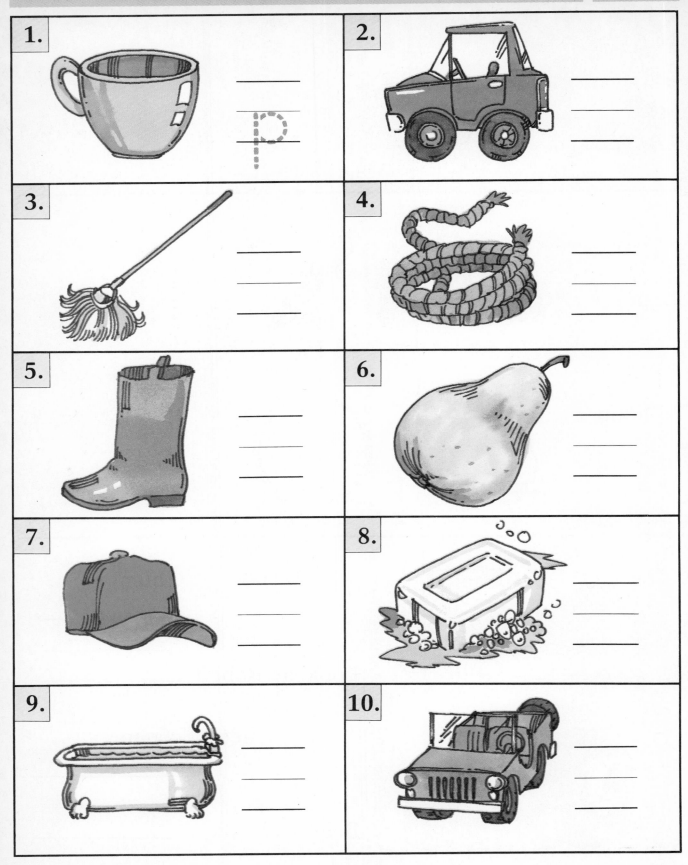

1.

p

2.

3.

4.

5.

6.

7.

8.

9.

10.

Decoding/Phonics: End Sound *p*
Listen as I name each picture. (Name the picture in each box.) Now trace or print the letter *p* for any picture whose name *ends* with the sound for *p*.

DRUMS

Houghton Mifflin Reading, 1989 Edition

| yes | no |

1. Did Mother make soup?

_____
_____

2. Is it for John?

_____
_____
_____

3. Is the kite Pam wants red?

_____
_____
_____

4. Will it work now?

_____
_____
_____

Vocabulary: "Fox Gets Lunch" (Part Two)
Read each question and look at the picture. If the answer to the question is *yes*, print *yes*. If the answer is *no*, print *no*.

DRUMS

| Fox   Mother   Rabbit |

1. I think a fox is a frog.

   _____

   _____

2. I make fly soup for the fox.

   _____

   _____

3. I like rabbits for lunch.

   _____

   _____

4. I do not like fly soup!

   _____

   _____

Comprehension: "Fox Gets Lunch" (Part Two)   DRUMS
The sentences on this page are about "Fox Gets Lunch." Read each sentence. Decide which animal it
tells about, and print your answer. The animals' names are at the top of the page. You will need to use
one name twice.   Houghton Mifflin Reading, 1989 Edition

1. We like the big bears.

2. You will want to see the pigs.

3. The bear will go home now.

4. The frogs will go in.

5. A frog will surprise the pig.

6. Some homes are here now.

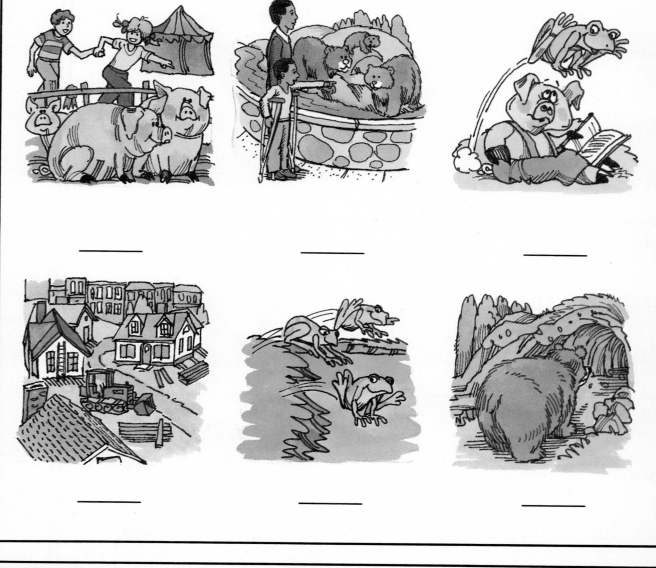

Decoding: Plurals

Read the sentences. Then look at the pictures. Decide which picture goes with each sentence. Write the number of the sentence below its picture.

DRUMS

Houghton Mifflin Reading, 1989 Edition

1.

Bug   Both   Beach

_____ kites are good.

2.

path   patch   peach

I will take this _____ .

3.

thumb   hum   tub

My _____ is red now.

4.

crop   chop   hop

Will you help me _____ ?

5.

book   beat   beach

It's fun at the _____ !

Decoding/Phonics: Digraphs *ch, th* (Initial and Final)   DRUMS
One word is missing from each sentence on this page. Complete the sentence so that it tells about the picture. Circle the word you would use.

Houghton Mifflin Reading, 1989 Edition

1.

Ana will go home with Pam for lunch.

Ana likes soup.

Pam wants to make what Ana likes.

What will Pam do?

_____ Pam will not make lunch.

_____ Pam will make soup for lunch.

2.

John wants Ana to come out now.

Ana needs to do some work.

John likes to help out.

What will John do?

_____ John will help Ana with the work.

_____ John will look for a kite.

3.

The rabbit sees the fox.

The fox would like the rabbit for lunch.

The rabbit would not like to be lunch.

What will the rabbit do?

_____ It will help the fox.

_____ It will go where the fox can't see it.

Comprehension: Predicting Outcomes
Read each story and the question below it. Decide which sentence answers the question. Put an X by the sentence.

DRUMS

Houghton Mifflin Reading, 1989 Edition

1

- ( ) too
- ( ) no
- ( ) now

- ( ) this
- ( ) your
- ( ) yes

- ( ) red
- ( ) did
- ( ) get

2

- ( ) not
- ( ) more
- ( ) mother

- ( ) tell
- ( ) little
- ( ) this

- ( ) come
- ( ) see
- ( ) some

3

- ( ) day
- ( ) make
- ( ) may

- ( ) fox
- ( ) frog
- ( ) find

- ( ) with
- ( ) where
- ( ) the

4

- ( ) soup
- ( ) help
- ( ) some

- ( ) will
- ( ) tail
- ( ) tell

- ( ) little
- ( ) like
- ( ) lunch

Vocabulary Test
Find number 1. Look at the words in the first box. Find the word *no*. Mark the space for the word. (Continue in this manner, pronouncing the words to be tested.)

DRUMS

Houghton Mifflin Reading, 1989 Edition

The Surprise Hat

by Patricia Demuth

Pig: Bear, you have a BIG hat!
I like it.

Bear: Do you want a big hat, Pig?

Pig: Yes, I do.
My hat is too tiny.

Bear: Here, Pig.
You may have my hat.

Houghton Mifflin Reading, 1989 Edition

Pig: But, Bear!

Look at you now!

You still have a hat!

Bear: Did I surprise you, Pig?

Pig: Yes, you did!

Bear: Here comes Turtle.

I will surprise Turtle, too.

Turtle: What big hats you have!

Bear: You do not have a hat, Turtle.
Here! You may have my hat.

Turtle: You still have a hat, Bear.

That surprises me!

Pig: It surprises me, too!

Do you have more hats, Bear?

Bear: You will see.

Here comes Fox.

Houghton Mifflin Reading, 1989 Edition

Bear: Do you like my hat, Fox?

Fox: Yes, I do.

I would like a hat like that.

Bear: Take it, Fox.

This hat is for you.

Fox: Oh, look!

You still have a hat, Bear!

But it is tiny.

Bear: My hat is tiny?

Houghton Mifflin Reading, 1989 Edition

Fox: Yes, Bear, it is.

Pig has a big, big hat.

Turtle has a big hat, too.

My hat is not too big.

But your hat is tiny.

Pig: This is a day for surprises.

Your surprises were fun, Bear.

Bear: Now the surprise is on me.

I had a big hat.

But now I have a tiny hat.